Louis Armstrong, Jazz Artist

by Maya Davis

PEARSON

Scott
Foresman

Editorial Offices: Glenview, Illinois • Parsippany, New Jersey • New York, New York
Sales Offices: Needham, Massachusetts • Duluth, Georgia • Glenview, Illinois
Coppell, Texas • Sacramento, California • Mesa, Arizona

Jazz was created in New Orleans and was spread north by musicians traveling up the Mississippi River. Jazz became very popular in cities like Chicago and New York City.

New Orleans Jazz and Louis Armstrong

In the early 1900s, something very exciting was happening in the city of New Orleans, Louisiana. A new kind of music was being played in the parts of town where many African Americans lived. This new kind of music was called *jazz.*

Jazz sounded like other kinds of African American music that were popular. It could have a slow, heavy beat, like *the blues.* It could have a quick, lively tempo, like *ragtime.* Jazz also sounded like the marching band music so often heard in New Orleans.

---

beat: rhythm, driving force

tempo: rate of speed of a musical piece

But jazz had its own sound. Musicians who played jazz improvised, making up the music as they went along. They did not use sheet music—in fact, many of them could not read music at all.

Louis Armstrong was born in New Orleans at about the same time that jazz was developing. He would grow up to be one of the great jazz artists of the twentieth century. He made music with the trumpet and his own voice.

This is what sheet music looks like.

sheet music: music printed on sheets of paper

Louis playing his trumpet at the Savoy Hotel in Britain

As an adult, Louis traveled the world, taking jazz to Europe, Asia, and Africa. He performed before kings, queens, and world leaders. People all over the world called him affectionately by his nickname, "Satchmo." This was short for "satchel mouth," a nickname his childhood friends had given him because they said his mouth was so big.

The beginning of his life was not so happy. In fact, it was difficult, as the lives of many African Americans were at the time.

---

satchel: small bag for carrying things

Louis Armstrong was born in this house, at 723 Jane Alley, New Orleans.

Childhood

Louis Armstrong was born on August 4, 1901, in one of the poorest neighborhoods in New Orleans. His mother was fifteen years old when he was born. His father left the family three weeks after Louis was born. For the first five years of his life, Louis lived with his grandmother.

Louis's grandmother worked washing laundry, but she made very little money. She could afford only the simplest food—rice or beans. Louis never wore shoes. The clothes he wore were old and ragged.

When Louis was five years old, he went to live with his mother. The neighborhood where Louis's mother lived was poorer than his grandmother's neighborhood.

---

ragged: torn or worn out

When Louis was six years old, he began attending the Fisk School for Boys. Louis went to school there until he finished third grade.

Louis also started working when he was six years old. He worked for a family that had a wagon and sold coal in the neighborhood. This was hard work for a young child, but it took Louis all over the neighborhood. He heard the music that was coming out of places where grown-ups danced and listened to music. He heard ragtime and the blues, but more and more, he heard jazz.

Louis also heard music from the riverboats on the Mississippi River. These boats had bands and dance halls.

Louis heard Joseph "King" Oliver playing a cornet like this.

Soon, Louis had a favorite performer. It was Joseph "King" Oliver, a cornet player in a popular band. Louis began to dream of playing the cornet too. But first he would have to buy a cornet. This was hard, because all the money he earned went to support his family.

Louis started a singing group with three of his friends to make extra money. The group sang on street corners for tips. Louis saved $5 and bought a used cornet.

Louis enjoyed making music. He also had a natural talent for playing his cornet *by ear*—listening to a song and then imitating it perfectly.

But on New Year's Eve 1912, Louis got in trouble with some boys. A policeman arrested him. Louis was sent to a school for African American boys who got into trouble.

---

cornet: a horn similar to a trumpet but slightly smaller

Louis played in the band at the school.

Louis was afraid of going to the school. But once he got there, he realized the school was not so bad. The school was shabby and had little money, but there was always enough food. The rules were strict. The boys were given jobs. Life was orderly and regular. Louis liked this way of life. Best of all, the school had a band.

Louis joined the band as soon as he could. This gave him a chance to get formal training in music. The band director, Peter Davis, showed him how to play the tambourine and the bass drum. Louis played these instruments easily. Finally, Davis gave Louis a horn. In a very short time, Louis showed dramatic improvement. He was playing harmony to any melody the band played. Soon he was the leader of the band.

Louis spent about eighteen months at the school. When he was released, he kept playing the cornet.

---

shabby: in poor condition

harmony: musical notes played at the same time as the main musical notes in a piece of music

melody: the main musical notes or tune in a piece of music

King Oliver's Creole Jazz Band was made up of the best New Orleans jazz musicians. When Louis (center) joined it, the band became a sensation in Chicago.

Musician

Louis got a job playing cornet at a dance hall. Little by little, Louis got good enough at his cornet to play with different bands around the city. Eventually, he became friends with the cornet player he had admired years before, King Oliver.

Oliver could see that Louis had talent. Louis could play jazz very well with his cornet. Oliver let Louis take his place when he wanted a rest from playing. He also recommended Louis for jobs with other bands.

In 1918, Oliver left New Orleans to perform in Chicago. When Oliver left, Louis took his place as the jazz trombonist and bandleader, in Kid Ory's band. In 1922, Oliver asked Louis to come to Chicago to join his Creole Jazz Band.

---

trombonist: person who plays the trombone

Louis Armstrong (right) performs with his first music teacher, Peter Davis.

In 1924, Louis moved to New York City to play with the Fletcher Henderson Orchestra. It was the top African American band of the time. During this time, Louis began to play the trumpet instead of the cornet. He also began to sing.

African American jazz musicians faced prejudice almost everywhere they went. Often, they could not use the front door of the places they played in. When they traveled, often they could not stay at hotels or eat at restaurants—those places served only white people. Later in his life, Louis spoke out against prejudice and racism.

---

racism: a belief that one race of humans is better than other races

Louis came back to Chicago in 1925 and formed his own bands. He recorded and performed at the Savoy Ballroom. His performances were broadcast live on the radio all across the country. In the 1930s, Louis was the first African American to host a nationally broadcast radio show.

Over the next forty years, Louis became world-famous. He had a friendly, easy-going personality that audiences loved. The United States government named him "Ambassador Satch." He performed in concerts all over the world to spread good will for America. Louis also appeared in over thirty movies and on television shows.

Louis teaches children to play the trumpet.

Wonderful Artist

Louis died in his sleep on July 6, 1971. Since his death, he has been honored in many ways. He is recognized by new generations of musicians and fans as one of the founding fathers of jazz.

In a song he recorded toward the end of his life, "What a Wonderful World," Louis sings about the beauty and love in the world. The message of the song is simple. The world and its people are full of beautiful colors, life, and love. There is much to be joyful about in this wonderful world.

Louis made his music with this sense of joy. He felt jazz in his heart.

Is there a kind of music that you feel in your heart?